CRAFT BOX

VICTORIAN TIMES

12 projects to make and do

Published in 2014 by Wayland
Copyright © Wayland 2014

Wayland
338 Euston Road
London NW1 3BH

Wayland Australia
Level 17/207 Kent Street
Sydney, NSW 2000

Editor: Elizabeth Brent
Designer: Rocket Design (East Anglia) Ltd
Craft stylist: Annalees Lim
Photographer: Simon Pask, N1 Studios
Proofreader/indexer: Susie Brooks

Picture acknowledgements:
All step-by-step craft photography: Simon Pask, N1 Studios; images
used throughout for creative graphics: Shutterstock.

A cataloguing record for this title is available at the British Library.
Dewey number: 941.081-dc23

ISBN: 978 0 7502 8419 6

10 9 8 7 6 5 4 3 2 1

First published in 2013 by Wayland

Printed in China

Wayland is a division of Hachette Children's Books,
an Hachette UK company.
www.hachette.co.uk

Contents

the
Victorians

The Victorians were people who lived in Britain during the reign of Queen Victoria, which lasted for more than sixty years. Among them were many great engineers and inventors. Victorian inventions include the light bulb, the telephone and railways. The first cameras and music players, such as phonographs, gramophones and barrel organs, were also made in Victorian times.

Queen Victoria reigned from 1837–1901

During the Victorian era, there were many great explorers and plant collectors who returned from their travels around the world to write books and give lectures about their discoveries. Famous Victorians included the scientist Charles Darwin, the engineer Isambard Kingdom Brunel and the writer Charles Dickens.

The Victorians were skilled at many arts and crafts. Craftsmen learned their trades as apprentices, working with materials such as wood, glass, metal and leather, to become cabinet or glassmakers, blacksmiths and tanners. Some worked as journeymen and travelled around the country to find work.

Others ran their own workshops, employing apprentices and journeymen. Crafts were also popular pastimes. Women who had money and time practised home crafts like needle and beadwork, lace making and paper crafts.

Victorian buildings and objects can tell us lots of fascinating facts about how the Victorians lived, from the things they used in their homes to the way they dressed and the games they played as pastimes. Be inspired by the Victorians to make some Victorian crafts of your own!

make a
Penny Black

The first adhesive postage stamp was introduced in May 1840. For the first time, people could send letters any distance for one penny. The 'Penny Black' stamp was printed in black ink and showed the head of Queen Victoria.

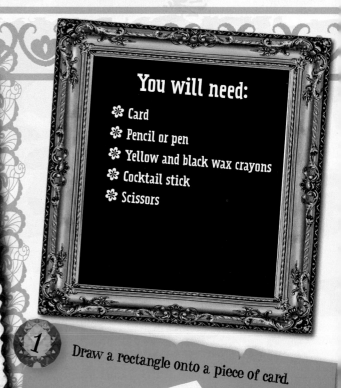

You will need:
* Card
* Pencil or pen
* Yellow and black wax crayons
* Cocktail stick
* Scissors

 Draw a rectangle onto a piece of card.

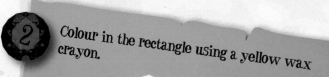 Colour in the rectangle using a yellow wax crayon.

 Go over the yellow base thoroughly using a black wax crayon.

4

Using a cocktail stick, scratch in the profile of the Queen's head, and small squares at each corner of the rectangle.

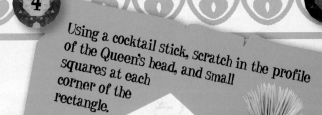

5

Using the lines as your guide, scratch away the black crayon to add detail to the Queen's head. Scratch away the black from the yellow squares at the top to make patterns, and at the bottom to make an M and an H.

6

Scratch away a criss-cross pattern down each side of the stamp between the squares, then scratch the word 'POSTAGE' at the top of the stamp and 'ONE PENNY' at the bottom and cut the stamp out.

Did you know...
Penny Black stamps were printed in big sheets, the letters at the bottom of each stamp showed where in the sheet it had come from.

make a Barrel organ

Barrel or 'monkey' organs were a popular street entertainment in Victorian times. They were pushed around the streets on handcarts and played tunes when the organ grinder turned the handle. Monkeys were trained to attract an audience and collect money.

You will need:

❊ Small cardboard box
❊ Scissors
❊ Grey paper or card
❊ Strong card
❊ Narrow cardboard tubes
❊ Glue
❊ Gold paint
❊ Brushes
❊ Coloured paper
❊ Gold card
❊ Scraps of gift wrap/cards

1 Turn the box on its side and cut away a window. Cut a piece of grey card and stick it to the side of the box opposite the window.

2 Cut a piece of strong card the depth and width of the box that will fit inside it behind the window.

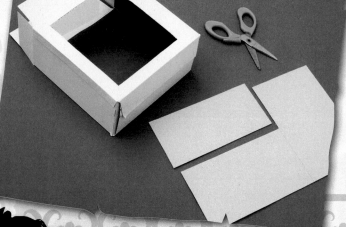

3 Cut the cardboard tubes to different lengths, and stick them onto the card with the tallest in the middle. Paint them gold.

4 Cover the box in coloured paper, and cut four pieces of gold card to frame the window edges.

5 Slide in the tubes so they show through the window, then glue the box shut. Decorate the sides and top by gluing on scraps cut from gift wrap and cards.

Did you know...
Tunes were encoded in pins and staples onto a wooden barrel that revolved inside the organ.

make a
Silhouette portrait

Silhouettes were a popular form of portrait in Victorian times. Women enjoyed making silhouettes as 'keepsakes' for loved ones, and people paid silhouette artists to make their portraits at fairs.

You will need:

❀ Digital/phone camera
❀ Printer and paper
❀ Tracing paper
❀ Pencil
❀ Sticky tape
❀ Black construction paper
❀ Scissors
❀ Card in two colours
❀ Serrated craft scissors
❀ Glue

1 Take a photograph showing the head and shoulders of your subject in side view. Print it onto ordinary printer paper to make an image about 6cm high.

2 Trace around the profile onto a piece of tracing paper.

3 Tape the tracing paper onto the black construction paper and carefully cut around the outline, cutting away the shoulders in a curved line.

4 Cut an oval 10cm long from white or pale-coloured card.

5 Glue the oval to a piece of card in a contrasting colour and cut around it using the serrated scissors, leaving a margin of 1cm.

6 Glue the silhouette in the middle of the smaller oval.

Did you know...

Skilled silhouette artists could cut a profile in a few minutes 'by eye'. Another method was to use a candle or lamp to project a shadow of the subject's profile onto a white background.

make a
Bellows camera

Photography was invented in Victorian times. Cameras were made from wood and brass with folding leather bellows that opened and shut as the photographer adjusted the lens. As cameras were expensive to buy, people went to portrait studios to have their photograph taken.

You will need:

❀ Cardboard tea box
❀ Corrugated card
❀ Scissors
❀ Glue
❀ Brown paint
❀ Brush
❀ Black construction paper
❀ Ruler
❀ Acetate
❀ Gold card

1 Cut two squares of corrugated card the same width as the box. Cut away a circle from one and a square from the other. Glue the squares to the open lid of the box.

2 Paint the box and card brown.

3 Cut three strips of construction paper the same width as your camera but three times its length. 'Concertina' them by folding them backwards and forwards.

Stick a piece of acetate behind the circular hole. To make the bellows, feed the creases of the concertina-folded paper into each other to make a U shape. Glue them in place, then stick them into the space between the box and the card.

Glue a ring of gold card around the circle on the front of the camera. Cut strips and other shapes from the card and glue them to the camera to form the brass trim along the front and sides.

Did you know...
Victorian photographers had to adjust the lens to focus the picture and fix it onto a glass plate using chemicals. Portrait sitters had to stay still for up to half an hour while the photographer worked.

make a
Spinning top

Many Victorian toys were made from wood, ranging from homemade peg dolls to alphabet bricks, Noah's Arks and rocking horses. Popular wooden toys included hoops that were rolled along with a stick, and colourful spinning tops.

1 Glue the bowls together around the rims.

2 Use the felt tips to decorate the bowls. Start your design at the centre and work outwards as this will look good when the top spins.

3 Push the pencil point through the centre of both bowls so that about 3cm of pencil is showing at the bottom.

4

Paint the Styrofoam ball.

5

Push the ball onto the top end of the pencil and glue it in place.

Did you know...
Many Victorian toys were still crafted by hand, but factories were beginning to produce the first tin and clockwork toys.

make a
Victorian police helmet

Victorian policemen wore helmets made from black felt with a brass badge and crown on the front. These replaced the leather top hats worn by London's Metropolitan Police force, which was set up in 1829 by Sir Robert Peel.

1 Cut a strip of card 7cm wide, and long enough to go around your head plus 5cm. Bend it into a circle and tape the ends together to form a head band.

2 Cut strips of card measuring 50cm by 5cm. Staple one strip across the head band and another over it to form a cross. Then staple another strip across them to form a star.

3 Cut four pointed arch shapes the same height as the frame from the black felt. Cut a slit from the top to the middle of each piece and glue the felt shapes to the card frame.

Fill in any gaps with more black felt, and cut away the sides of the head band to make the front and back pointed.

Cut four strips from the edge of the plate and glue them to the top of the helmet in a cross-shape. Glue a ball of gold foil to the top of the cross. Cut a big circle, small circle and a square from the plate and glue them to the front of the helmet.

6

Cut two lengths of fringe trim and glue them around the front and sides of the helmet.

Did you know...
Victorian policemen carried a stick or 'truncheon', handcuffs and a wooden rattle they could use to summon help.

make a
Jubilee souvenir

Queen Victoria reigned for more than 60 years, celebrating her Silver, Golden and Diamond Jubilees. The colour of pressed amber glass made it popular for Golden Jubilee souvenirs such as glass dishes, plates and baskets.

You will need:
❀ Large paper plate
❀ Pencil
❀ Yellow cellophane
❀ Marker pen
❀ Scissors
❀ Glue
❀ Glitter glue

1 Draw a crown in the middle of the plate using the pencil. Draw a ring of laurel leaves and a circle around it.

2 Draw around the plate onto the cellophane and cut out a circle slighter larger to leave a margin of about 1cm all round.

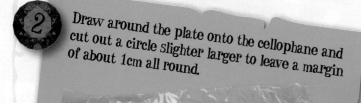

3 Glue the cellophane onto the plate.

18

4

Cut around the edges of the plate to make a scalloped edge.

5

Write 'THE QUEEN'S JUBILEE' in glitter glue around the edge of the plate and the dates 1837 and 1887 above and below the crown.

6

Use glitter glue to go over the crown and laurel wreath.

Did you know...

Every kind of souvenir was made to celebrate Queen Victoria's Jubilee years, from beer and biscuit barrels to playing cards and moustache cups.

make a
Model of the Crystal Palace

The Crystal Palace was built in London's Hyde Park in 1851 to house the Great Exhibition, which showcased the best designs and inventions of the time. It was designed by Sir Joseph Paxton and built from cast iron and glass.

1 Arrange three boxes on their sides with the largest at the bottom and the smallest at the top. Glue them together.

2 Cut two semicircles of card, narrower than the long sides of the smallest box, and glue one onto each side.

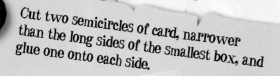

3 Paint the boxes using white acrylic paint.

20

4 Make two window patterns and a zigzag template by sticking string to pieces of cardboard.

5 Press the string templates into black paint and print them onto the sides of the boxes, starting at the bottom and working up.

6 Use a marker pen to decorate the top arch and fill in any detail.

Did you know...
The Crystal Palace was moved to a new site after the Exhibition, but it burned down in 1936.

make a Victorian calling card

When Victorians visited family or friends, they would take their 'calling cards'. In well-off households, these were taken in by servants on silver or china trays to announce visitors. Cards were hand-painted with landscape scenes, flowers or birds and trimmed with ribbons or feathers.

You will need:
- ✿ Gold or coloured card
- ✿ Ruler
- ✿ Scissors
- ✿ Feathers
- ✿ Glue
- ✿ Gift wrap
- ✿ White paper
- ✿ Pen

1 Cut one piece of card measuring 10cm by 6cm and one measuring 7cm by 6cm.

2 Cut two feathers to 6cm high and glue them to either side of the back of the smaller piece of card.

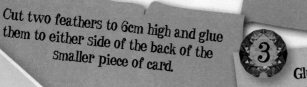

3 Glue the front of the larger piece of card and press the back of the feathered card down on to it.

4

Cut out two rectangles of gift wrap, slightly smaller than the front piece of card. Trim one to make it even smaller, cut off the corners and stick it to the other piece of paper. Stick both to the front piece of card.

5 Cut a piece of white paper, write your name on it and stick it to the front piece of card.

Victoria

Did you know...
A fold at the top right corner of a card meant it had been brought in person, not by a servant.

6

Use more gift wrap to make a flap big enough to hide your name, then stick it by one edge to the front piece of card, over your name.

make a
Terrarium

Terrariums, glass cases for growing and displaying plants, were popular in Victorian homes. Victorian plant collectors travelled around the world bringing back new plants. Many collected ferns, which became popular house plants.

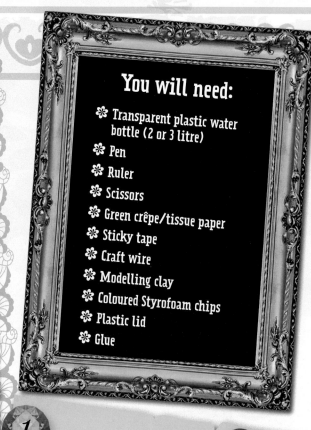

You will need:

- ❀ Transparent plastic water bottle (2 or 3 litre)
- ❀ Pen
- ❀ Ruler
- ❀ Scissors
- ❀ Green crêpe/tissue paper
- ❀ Sticky tape
- ❀ Craft wire
- ❀ Modelling clay
- ❀ Coloured Styrofoam chips
- ❀ Plastic lid
- ❀ Glue

1

Draw a line around the bottle, about 10cm from the top, then cut around the line.

2 Cut four strips of crêpe and tissue paper 30cm long by 4cm wide. Fold each strip backwards and forwards in concertina folds.

3 Cut the top of each strip into a triangle shape, and snip one edge of each triangle to make a fringe.

4

Open out each strip and hold along the bottom edge, then bunch and tape the leaves together.

Did you know...
Terrariums were also called Wardian cases after Nathaniel Ward, the man who invented them.

5

Stick some craft wire to the taped ends and open out the leaves. Fill the neck of the bottle with modelling clay and push the craft wires into it.

6

Place the bottle neck onto the plastic lid. Chop up the Styrofoam chips and glue them all over the bottle neck so you can't see any plastic. Place the bottom half of the bottle over the ferns.

25

make a
Candlestick telephone

The telephone was invented in the 1870s by Alexander Graham Bell with the help of his assistant, an electrician called Thomas Watson. By the 1890s, early box telephones had been replaced by candlestick telephones, made from wood or brass.

You will need:

* Strong narrow cardboard tubes
* Scissors
* Cardboard
* Modelling clay
* Ice cream sticks
* Glue
* Paper/foam cup
* Tape
* 80g food can
* Gold metallic paint
* Black acrylic paint
* Brushes
* Gold cord

1 Cut a piece about 6cm long from the tube and stand the longer part in a lump of modelling clay. Cut a piece of card to make a base and glue it onto the clay.

2 Cut an ice cream stick in half and stick one half to either side of the tube, just below the top.

3 Cut down a cup and tape it to the end of the short tube. Cut a cardboard ring the same diameter as the cup, and a cardboard circle a bit wider than the tube. Glue the ring to the cup and the circle to the tube.

4 Cut a cardboard circle wider than base. Glue it to the cardboard underneath the modelling clay. Glue the food can to the top of the tube.

5 Paint the long tube, the ice cream sticks, the modelling clay and the cup gold. Paint the can, the cardboard base, the short tube and the card circle black.

6 Cut a piece of gold cord. Push one end into the modelling clay and glue the other end to the cardboard circle on top of the short tube.

Did you know...
The earliest telephones had no dial. Telephone operators took calls and put callers through to a number.

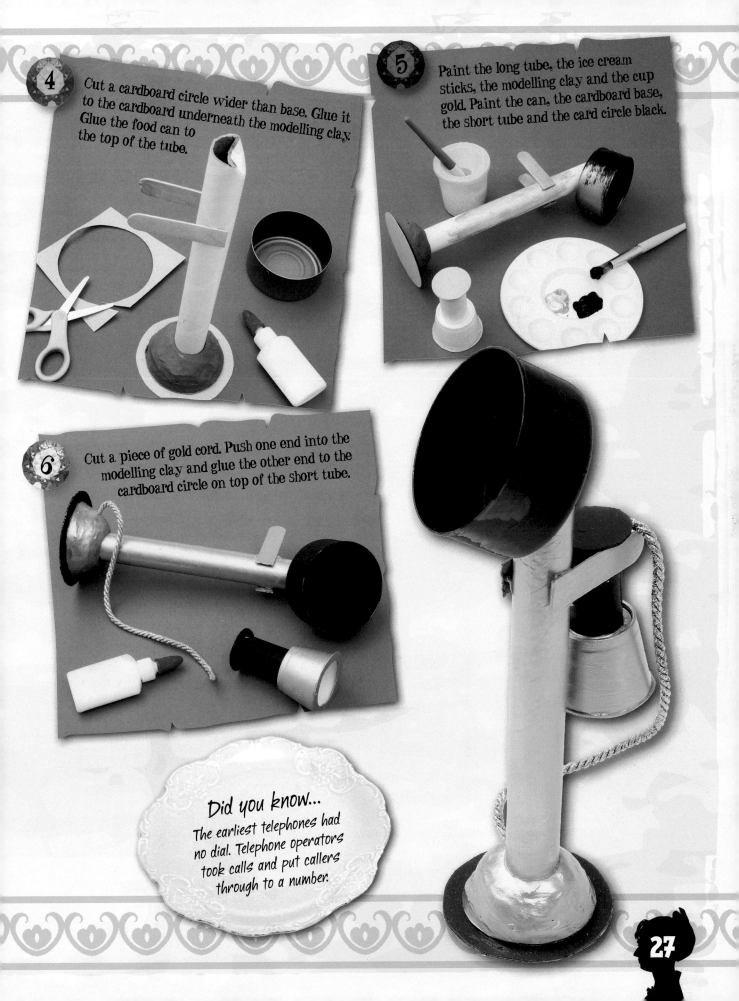

make a Cornucopia

Queen Victoria's husband Prince Albert introduced the fashion for Christmas trees from Germany to Britain. Families made their own paper tree decorations including cornucopias, decorative cones that held sweets and treats.

You will need:
- ❄ Green or red card
- ❄ Scissors
- ❄ Ruler
- ❄ Glue
- ❄ Christmas cards/gift wrap
- ❄ Glitter glue
- ❄ Hole punch
- ❄ Coloured wool/ribbon

1 Cut a 20cm square of coloured card.

2 Roll the card into a cone shape and glue the edges shut.

3 Cut out scraps from Christmas cards and gift wrap, collecting images like holly leaves, Christmas greetings and snowflakes.

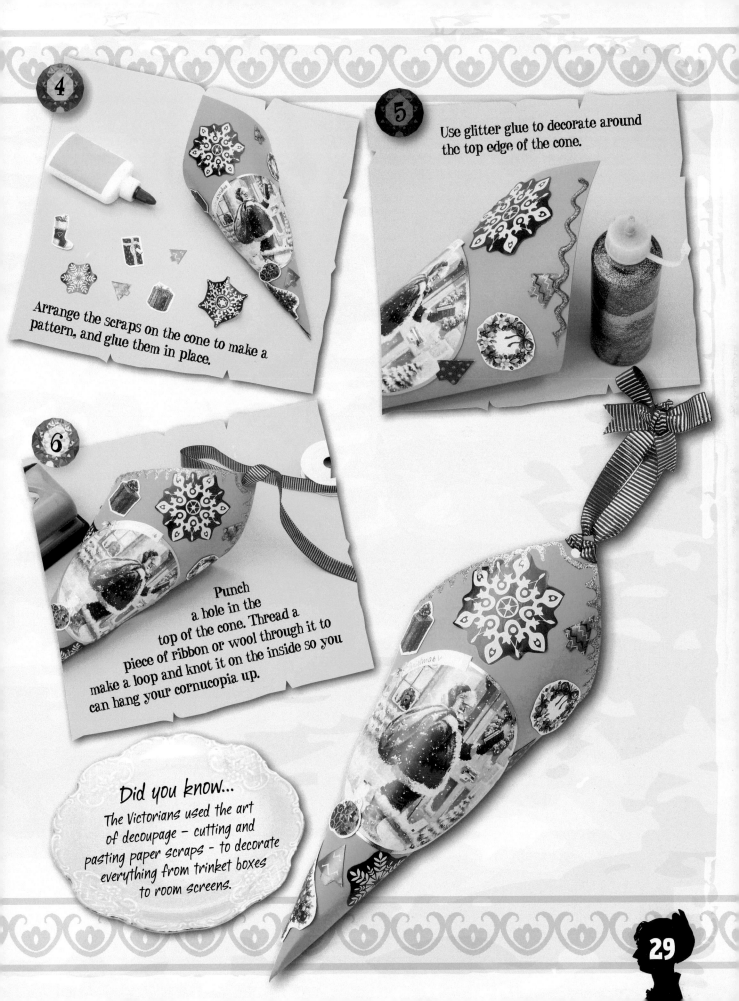

4 Arrange the scraps on the cone to make a pattern, and glue them in place.

5 Use glitter glue to decorate around the top edge of the cone.

6 Punch a hole in the top of the cone. Thread a piece of ribbon or wool through it to make a loop and knot it on the inside so you can hang your cornucopia up.

Did you know...
The Victorians used the art of decoupage — cutting and pasting paper scraps — to decorate everything from trinket boxes to room screens.

Glossary

Adhesive Sticky.

Amber A yellow or reddish-brown colour.

Apprentice A trainee learning a skilled trade or craft.

Barrel organ A large instrument that plays music when its handle is turned.

Bellows On an old-fashioned camera, the collapsible part with folds in it that connects the body of the camera to the lens.

Cabinet A piece of furniture with shelves or doors, used for displaying or containing things.

Clockwork A mechanism that works using gears and a spring, and must be wound up.

Encode To convert something into code.

Engineer Someone who designs and builds the working parts of engines, machines or buildings.

Felt A fabric formed by pressing wool fibres together.

Ferns Flowerless plants with feathery leaves.

Gramophone A type of old-fashioned record player.

Handcart A small cart that can be pulled or pushed by hand.

Inventor A person who invents things.

Journeyman An assistant craftsman, sometimes hired by the day.

Jubilee A special anniversary of the accession to the throne of a king or queen.

Landscape A painting or drawing of the countryside.

Moustache cup A cup with a ledge inside, used by men to keep their moustaches dry whilst drinking.

Phonograph An early type of gramophone.

Portrait A painting of a person.

Silhouette The profile of a person, drawn or cut out in black paper.

Souvenir Something that is bought as a reminder of an occasion or place.

Tanner A person whose job is to tan leather.

Trinket A small ornament or piece of jewellery.

Further information

BOOKS

A Victorian Childhood by Ruth Thomson (Franklin Watts, 2013)

Explore! Victorians by Jane Bingham (Wayland, 2014)

History From Objects: The Victorians by Angela Royston (Wayland, 2012)

History Relived: The Victorians by Alison Cooper (Wayland, 2012)

Men, Women and Children in Victorian Times by Peter Hepplewhite (Wayland, 2012)

The Gruesome Truth About the Victorians by Jillian Powell (Wayland, 2012)

WEBSITES

http://www.bbc.co.uk/schools/primaryhistory/victorian_britain
This BBC website is designed for KS2 learning.

http://homeworkhelp.stjohnssevenoaks.com/victorians.html
This brilliant website from Woodlands Junior School is packed full of information about The Victorians.

http://www.nationalarchives.gov.uk/victorians/
This National Archives website includes activities and downloadable teacher's notes.

http://www.bl.uk/learning/histcitizen/victorians/victorianhome.html
Learn all about the lives of ordinary Victorians on this website from the British Library.

Index